MARY FORD
COOKIES
for all Occasions

Select Editions

Author

Mary Ford is an extremely well-known name in cake artistry. She is a master cake decorator and teacher. Her step-by-step cake artistry books have sold over 600,000 copies world-wide. However, at heart Mary is concerned with a much wider field. Having run her own bakery business for many years, she remains an enthusiastic home-baker. This passionate interest resulted in her hugely successful book *Cake Recipes*.

This new book on baking reflects Mary's belief that anyone can bake, and that nothing beats the flavour of freshly made cookies and bars. Her unique step-by-step teaching method and practical hints mean that anyone can benefit from her many years of experience.

ACKNOWLEDGMENTS

Many thanks to:

Carmel Keens, who is the Senior Home Economist for Tate & Lyle Sugars, Great Britain. Carmel is a highly respected, and knowledgeable, figure in cookery circles. Her expertise is wide ranging, covering everything from cake decoration, recipe testing, new product development, to budget meals and health education in schools. She is sugar adviser to cookery editors, having produced many of the Tate & Lyle Sugars recipe leaflets and booklets. She is involved in travelling the country to attend trade shows and many major food exhibitions.

R & W Scott Ltd, Carluke, Scotland for providing all the chocolate used in this book.

Prestige Group U.K. plc, Egham, Surrey for supplying cake tins, cookware and decorating items used in this book.

First published in Canada in 2000 by:
Select Editions
8036 Enterprise Street
Burnaby, B.C. Canada V5A 1V7
Ph: (604) 415-2444 Fax: (604) 415-3444

© Copyright Mary Ford Publications Ltd, 1995

First published in Great Britain in 1995 by
Mary Ford Publications Ltd.,
a subsidiary of Michael O'Mara Holdings,
9 Lion Yard, Tremadoc Road, London SW4 7NQ, U.K..

ISBN 1-896639-11-9

Typesetting: Mitchell/Strange.
Printed in China.

CONTENTS

INGREDIENTS FOR COOKIES

Sugar, an essential ingredient in the kitchen, originates in the giant grass-like sugar cane which grows in tropical climates such as the Caribbean, Mauritius and Fiji. It is a flavour enhancer, preservative and natural sweetener as well as contributing to the texture of food.

Sugar can aptly be described as 'a taste of sunshine' because it is manufactured in plants as a direct result of the sun's energy, through a process known as photosynthesis. However, while all plants make sugars, commercially produced sugars are extracted only from sugar cane and sugar beet. These extraction processes remove undesirable impurities and produce the characteristic crystalline structure without the addition of any artificial colourings, flavourings or preservatives.

Nutritionally, brown and white sugars are virtually identical, but the distinctive colour and flavour of brown sugar arises from molasses, which is the syrup remaining after all the sugar has been removed from the cane juice. When manufacturing white sugar, the molasses is completely removed while the different brown sugars contain more, or less, of the syrup depending on the flavour and colour required. Therefore, careful selection of the type of sugar used can greatly enhance the finished taste and texture .

Confectioner's or Icing Sugar: is the finest of all sugars. It dissolves rapidly and is especially used in making icings, smooth toppings, confectionery, meringues and cake frostings. Apart from

decorating cakes, icing sugar is perfect for sweetening cold drinks and uncooked desserts, as its fine texture makes it easy to dissolve.

Granulated Sugar: has a very pure crystal and is an ideal boiling sugar. It can be used for sweetening tea, coffee, sprinkling over cereals or frosting cakes and glasses for decoration.

Superfine or Castor Sugar: is a free flowing sugar with very fine crystals. Excellent for use in baking cakes and other baked goods as the fine white grains ensure smooth blending and an even texture.

Corn Syrup: is an ideal sweetener and can be used in cooking and baking to add bulk, texture and taste. Light corn syrup is simply sweet, but dark corn syrup has a mild flavour of molasses. Dark would be better for most of these recipes.

Black Molasses: is a dark, viscous liquid with a characteristic flavour. It is obtained from cane molasses, a byproduct of sugar refining.

Demerara Sugar: This sugar has a golden colour with a unique flavour that makes it particularly popular in coffee. The grain is larger than granulated and is ideal for decorating biscuits and cakes, sprinkling over desserts and making crunchy toppings.

Light Brown Soft Sugar: This sugar is fine grained, creamy golden in colour and has a mild syrup flavour. It is best used when creamed with butter or margarine in any recipe that requires a deeper, richer colour and fuller flavour.

Dark Brown Soft Sugar: This sugar is darker with a strong flavour and is ideal for rich fruit cakes, gingerbread, spiced teabreads and puddings.

Self-raising Flour: If a recipe calls for 1 cup self-rising flour, you may substitute 1 cup (250 ml) all-purpose flour plus 1½ tbsp (22 ml) baking powder and ¼ tsp (1 ml) salt without a noticeable difference.

INTRODUCTION

I was delighted by the response to the publication of *Cake Recipes* and received numerous letters asking for a follow-up title. I have deliberately continued the successful step-by-step layout adopted in the previous book in this title and have incorporated the 'Mary's Tips' section which has been a popular feature.

As with *Cake Recipes*, I have collected my favourite cookie and bar recipes gathered over the years into one book. The recipes selected cater for all tastes and levels of experience in home baking. I have included many ideas which are suitable for children to make, watched over by an adult.

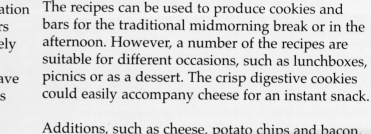

The recipes can be used to produce cookies and bars for the traditional midmorning break or in the afternoon. However, a number of the recipes are suitable for different occasions, such as lunchboxes, picnics or as a dessert. The crisp digestive cookies could easily accompany cheese for an instant snack.

Additions, such as cheese, potato chips and bacon, produce an interesting variety of tastes and textures from smooth to crunchy. A number of the recipes incorporate cooking chocolate, which is generally available in supermarkets and smaller stores. The range of toppings and decorations currently available provides ample opportunity for you to add your own original touches to the recipe.

In producing this book, I have worked closely with Carmel Keens (a home economist for a well-know sugar producer) and I pay tribute to her help in testing and helping with the recipes in this book.

All the recipes can be made with the most basic kitchen equipment. If you do not have exactly the right size of cake pan, you can vary the shape, so long as the overall area remains the same. In the same way, a variety of cutter shapes can be used to add your own variations to the finished product.

I am sure you agree that no commercially produced cookie can have quite the same taste and texture as a recipe made in your own kitchen or just out of the oven. I hope you will get as much enjoyment out of these recipes as I have and they provide many happy hours of baking and eating.

PASSION FRUIT SQUARES

INGREDIENTS
Makes 24

2 eggs, large		
Light brown soft sugar	125 ml	1/2 cup
Butter, melted	125 ml	1/2 cup
Carrots, peeled and grated	500 ml	2 cups
Banana, mashed	75 ml	1/3 cup
Cinnamon	5 ml	1 tsp
Nutmeg	5 ml	1 tsp
All spice	5 ml	1 tsp
Walnuts, chopped	125 ml	1/2 cup
Whole wheat flour	250 ml	1 cup
Baking powder	5 ml	1 tsp

TOPPING

Quark	125 ml	1/2 cup
Whipping cream	175 ml	3/4 cup
1 passion fruit (optional)		

DECORATION
Small carrots made from sugar paste or almond paste

CAKE PAN/COOKIE SHEET
Shallow cake pan, 18 x 28 cm, greased and lined with wax paper

BAKING
Preheated oven,
190° C or 375° F
Middle shelf
20 minutes, or until firm to touch

1. Whisk together the egg and sugar until thick and creamy, then whisk in the melted butter. Add the carrots, banana, spices and chopped walnuts. Mix together thoroughly.

2. Sift together the flour and baking powder, then gently fold into the mixture until well blended. Pour the mixture into the pan, spread evenly.

3. When baked, leave in tin for 10 minutes, then turn out to cool. Whisk Quark and cream together, then add scooped-out passion fruit. Spread over the top and cut into squares.

PEANUT CRISPS

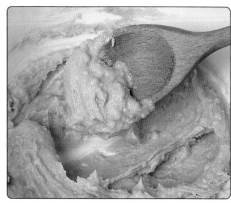

1. Thoroughly beat together the margarine, sugar, corn syrup and peanut butter.

2. Work in the sifted flour and oatmeal. Dissolve the baking soda in the hot water and stir into the mixture to form a soft dough.

INGREDIENTS
Makes 20

Margarine	60 ml	4 tbsp
Light brown soft sugar	60 ml	4 tbsp
Corn syrup	60 ml	4 tbsp
Crunchy peanut butter	125 ml	1/2 cup
All-purpose flour, sifted	175 ml	3/4 cup
Rolled oats	30 ml	2 tbsp
Baking soda	1 ml	1/4 tsp
Hot water	15 ml	1 tbsp

DECORATION
A little medium oatmeal

CAKE PAN/COOKIE SHEET
Cookie sheets, well greased

BAKING
Preheated oven,
 180° C or 360° F
Middle shelf
15 minutes, or until golden brown

3. Mould the mixture into a long roll, cut into 20 pieces, then mould into rounds. Space apart on sheets, flatten and sprinkle with a little oatmeal, then bake.

MARY'S TIPS
It is essential to measure the baking soda accurately to ensure perfect results.

CHECKERS

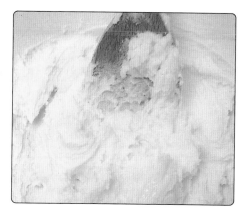

1. Beat the butter until soft and creamy, then beat in the sugar until light and fluffy.

2. Sift the flour into the creamed mixture and rub together to form a crumble texture. Divide the mixture into two equal portions, then mix the drinking chocolate into one portion.

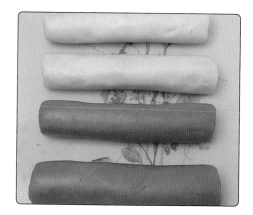

3. Continue mixing until crumbs bind together, adding a little more flour if necessary. Divide each portion into two and roll out to 20.5 cm long. Wrap in foil and chill until firm.

4. When chilled, cut each roll into four. Join alternate colours together using a little water. Cut into slices, place on sheets and bake.

INGREDIENTS
Makes 36

Butter or margarine	150 ml	3/5 cup
Sugar	125 ml	1/2 cup
All-purpose flour	500 ml	2 cups
Drinking chocolate powder	7 ml	1 1/2 tsp

CAKE PAN/COOKIE SHEET
Cookie sheets, well greased

BAKING
Preheated oven,
    180° C or 360° F
Middle shelf
8–10 minutes, or until just firm

BROWNIES

INGREDIENTS
Makes 24

Butter or margarine	125 ml	1/2 cup
Dark cooking chocolate	4 squares	4 squares
Dark brown soft sugar	125 ml	1/2 cup
Self-raising flour (see page 5)	175 ml	3/4 cup
Pinch of salt		
2 eggs, small		
Walnuts, chopped	125 ml	1/2 cup
Milk	15–30 ml	1–2 tbsp

TOPPING

Milk or dark cooking chocolate	4 squares	4 squares
Unsalted butter	60 ml	4 tbsp
1 egg, small		
Icing sugar, sifted	375 mL	1 1/2 cups

CAKE PAN/COOKIE SHEET
Shallow cake pan, 18 x 28 cm (7 x 11 ins), greased and lined with waxed paper

BAKING
Preheated oven,
180° C or 360° F
Middle shelf
30–40 minutes

MARY'S TIPS
A soft dropping consistency is when the mixture just drops off the spoon.
This rich, moist bar will store very well uncut in an airtight container.
If you are watching the calories, this bar is equally good without the topping.

1. Place the butter and chocolate together in a bowl over a saucepan of hot water and leave until melted. Remove from the heat and stir in the sugar. Leave to cool.

2. Sift the flour with the salt into a mixing bowl. Make a well in the centre and pour in the cooled chocolate mixture. Mix together thoroughly.

3. Beat in the eggs and walnuts. Stir in sufficient milk to give a soft dropping consistency. Spread mixture evenly in the pan and bake. Leave to cool in the pan.

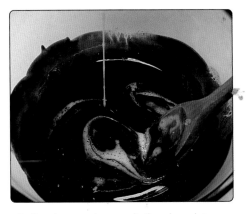

4. For the topping: melt the chocolate and butter in a pan over hot water, stirring occasionally (see below).

5. Thoroughly beat the egg and stir into the chocolate. Remove from the heat and stir in the icing sugar. Then beat well.

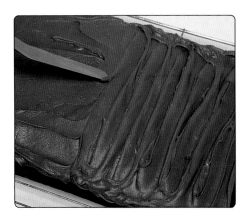

6. Leave to cool slightly until the mixture thickens. Place the base on a wire rack then spread the topping with a palette knife over the top. Cut into squares.

MELTING CHOCOLATE

This method should be used to melt chocolate flavoured coatings and cooking chocolates.

Melt the chocolate slowly on a very low heat, stirring gently. Stand the bowl over a saucepan which is small enough to support it without the bowl touching the base. The water should not be allowed to touch the bowl and the water should simmer, not boil.

Never try to hurry the melting process by turning up the heat.

When the chocolate is almost melted, remove from the heat and continue stirring until the chocolate is smooth and completely melted.

Keep it warm, stirring occasionally, to prevent it from setting while in use.

To melt cooking chocolate in a microwave:
Place 8 squares of broken dark cooking chocolate in a non-metallic bowl. Microwave for 4–5 minutes on a medium setting, stirring once.

When just softened, remove from the microwave oven and stir well until the chocolate has completely melted. It is important not to overheat beyond the point where the chocolate is just soft, as this makes it grainy and unmanageable.

Milk chocolate will need slightly less time.

WHISKY SNAPS

1. Melt the corn syrup, sugar and butter together gently in a saucepan. Stir in the whisky. Sift the flour and ground ginger together.

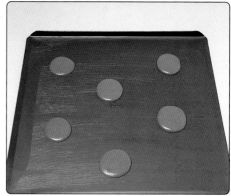

2. Mix all the ingredients together until well blended. Drop teaspoonfuls on to the sheets about 15 cm apart and bake.

INGREDIENTS
Makes 36

Corn syrup	75 ml	$^1/_3$ cup
Light brown soft sugar	125 ml	$^1/_2$ cup
Butter	125 ml	$^1/_2$ cup
Whisky	5 ml	1 tsp
All-purpose flour	250 ml	1 cup
Ground ginger	10 ml	2 tsp

FILLING
Whipping cream	310 ml	1$^1/_4$ cups

CAKE PAN/COOKIE SHEET
Cookie sheets, well greased

BAKING
Preheated oven,
  180° C or 360° F
Middle shelf
Approximately 10 minutes, or until golden
  brown

MARY'S TIPS
If the snaps cool too much
to roll around the spoon
handle, return them
to the oven to soften.

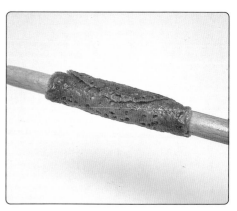

3. Immediately after baking, leave to cool for a few seconds before rolling round the greased handle of a large wooden spoon. Slide off and fill with whipped cream when cold.

STICKLEBACKS

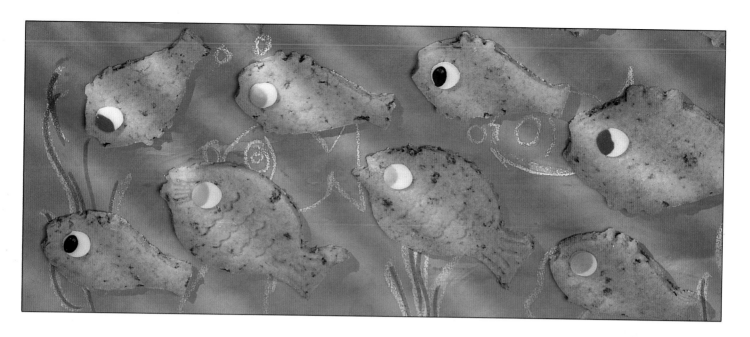

INGREDIENTS

All-purpose flour	175 ml	3/4 cup
Self-raising flour		
(see page 5)	175 ml	3/4 cup
Butter	125 ml	1/2 cup
Light brown soft sugar	60 ml	4 tbsp
Flaked bran cereal,		
crushed finely	30 ml	2 tbsp

DECORATION
A little piece of sugarpaste or royal icing
(see page 27) for the fish eyes

CAKE PAN/COOKIE SHEET
Cookie sheets, well greased

BAKING
Preheated oven,
    180° C or 360° F
Middle shelf
Approximately 20 minutes, or until
    golden brown

MARY'S TIPS
Place equal-sized fish
on each tray to keep
an even colour when baking.

1. Sift the flours into a bowl, then rub in the butter and sugar to give a breadcrumb mixture. Next add in the flaked bran cereal.

2. Knead together to form a smooth, well mixed dough.

3. Roll the mixture on a lightly floured surface. Cut out the fish, place on sheets and bake.

PEANUT CHEWS

INGREDIENTS
Makes 36

Butter	125 ml	1/2 cup
Low fat cream cheese	75 ml	1/3 cup
Vanilla extract	5 ml	1 tsp
Sugar	175 ml	3/4 cup
All-purpose flour	500 ml	2 cups
Pinch of salt		
Peanuts, finely chopped	250 ml	1 cup

CAKE PAN/COOKIE SHEET
Cookie sheets, well greased

BAKING
Preheated oven,
  190° C or 375° F
Middle shelf
Approximately 12 minutes, or until golden
  brown around the edges

MARY'S TIPS
Walnuts, finely chopped, can be substituted for peanuts.
This will give a stronger flavour.

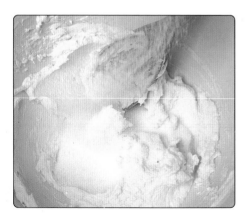

1. Blend the butter, cream cheese and vanilla extract together. Gradually beat in the sugar until light and creamy.

2. Sift the flour and salt together into the mixture, add the chopped peanuts, and blend to a soft dough.

3. Mould the dough into a roll and cut into 36 pieces. Mould into rounds, place on trays and flatten slightly before marking with a fork. After baking, leave on wire rack to cool.

LEMON FINGERS

1. Place all the ingredients in a mixing bowl and beat for 3 minutes on medium speed, or for 5 minutes by hand with a wooden spoon.

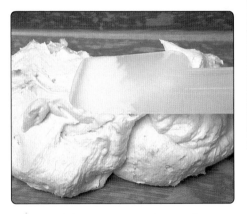

2. Spread the mixture evenly into the prepared pan and bake. After baking, place on a wire rack, remove the waxed paper and leave until cold.

3. For the topping: mix all the ingredients together to form a smooth, not too soft, icing. Spread over the sponge and leave to set before cutting. Decorate as required.

INGREDIENTS
Makes 25

Soft tub margarine	150 ml	3/5 cup
Sugar	160 ml	2/3 cup
Grated rind of 1 lemon		
3 eggs, small		
Self-raising flour		
(see page 5)	310 ml	1 1/4 cups

TOPPING
Icing sugar, sifted	425 ml	1 3/4 cups
Lemon juice	30 ml	2 tbsp
A little water		
Few drops of yellow colouring		

DECORATION
Lemons made from sugar paste
   or lemon slices

CAKE PAN/COOKIE SHEET
Shallow cake pan, 18 x 28 cm (7 x 11 ins),
   greased and lined with waxed paper

BAKING
Preheated oven,
   180° C or 360° F
Middle shelf
30–35 minutes

MARY'S TIPS
The grated rind and juice
of orange or lime can be used
to vary the flavour.
Decorate with sugar paste
limes or oranges.

GINGERBREAD MEN

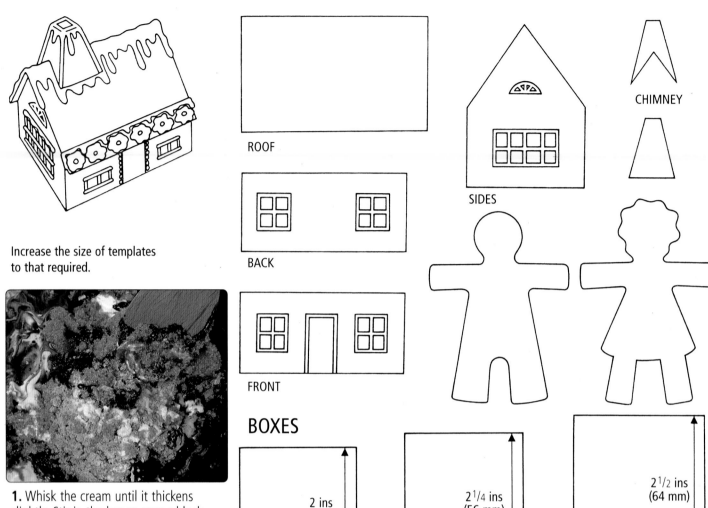

ROOF

BACK

FRONT

SIDES

CHIMNEY

Increase the size of templates to that required.

BOXES

2 ins
(50 mm)

2 ins
(50 mm)

2¼ ins
(56 mm)

2 ins
(50 mm)

2½ ins
(64 mm)

2¼ ins
(56 mm)

1. Whisk the cream until it thickens slightly. Stir in the brown sugar, black molasses, ginger, lemon rind and baking soda. Mix them well together.

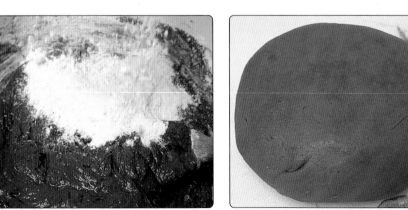

2. Immediately sift the flour into the mixture and gradually stir in.

3. Continue working in the flour until a smooth, pliable dough is formed. Roll out on lightly floured surface and cut out the pieces required using the templates as a guide.

4. Carefully place on the sheets, without distorting the shapes, then brush with water and bake. Remove from the sheets to cool. Then fix boxes together with royal icing and decorate.

GINGER STARS

INGREDIENTS
Makes 18

Margarine	75 ml	1/3 cup
Corn syrup	60 ml	4 tbsp
All-purpose flour	250 ml	1 cup
Ground ginger	5 ml	1 tsp

DECORATION
Small pieces of crystallized ginger

CAKE PAN/COOKIE SHEET
Cookie sheets, well greased

BAKING
Preheated oven,
　170° C or 340° F
Middle shelf
12–15 minutes, or until golden brown

MARY'S TIPS
These cookies can also be piped thinly in fingers and sandwiched together with ginger jam or buttercream (see page 81).

1. Cream the margarine and corn syrup together until blended. Sift the flour and ground ginger together and fold into the creamed mixture.

2. Place the mixture into a savoy bag with a large star piping tube, and pipe stars on the greased sheets. Top with crystallized ginger and bake.

APPLE FLAPJACKS

INGREDIENTS
Makes 12

Butter	125 ml	1/2 cup
Demerara sugar	125 ml	1/2 cup
Corn syrup	50 ml	3 tbsp
Rolled oats	625 ml	2 1/2 cups
Ground cinnamon	5 ml	1 tsp
1 cooking apple		

CAKE PAN/COOKIE SHEET
Shallow cake pan, 18 x 28 cm (7 x 11 ins),
  well greased

BAKING
Preheated oven,
  180° C or 360° F
Middle shelf
Approximately 20 minutes,
  or until flapjack is golden brown

MARY'S TIPS
A variety of ingredients can be
added to the basic mixture.
Try chopped or flaked nuts,
sesame seeds, dried fruit or
chocolate drops.

1. Melt the butter, sugar and corn syrup in a saucepan over low heat until the butter has just melted.

2. Stir in the rolled oats and cinnamon. Peel the apple and dice the flesh finely.

3. Stir apple into the flapjack until well blended. Press the mixture evenly into the pan and bake. After baking, allow to cool for 5 minutes, then mark into bars. Cut when cold.

HAZELNUT COOKIES

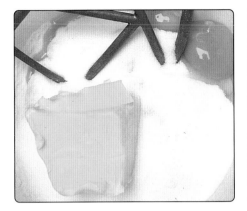

1. Place all the ingredients into a bowl and, using a beater on slow speed, blend together.

2. Remove from the bowl and gently knead together to form a smooth, firm dough. Leave to chill in the refrigerator for 1 hour.

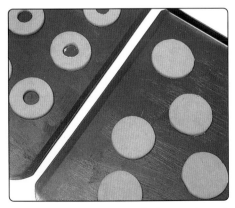

3. Roll out and cut into whole rounds and rings, then bake. When cold, fix together with jam or preserve, dust with icing sugar, and fill the tops with piping jelly.

INGREDIENTS
Makes 30

All-purpose flour, sifted	310 ml	1 1/4 cups
Butter	150 ml	3/5 cup
Sugar	160 ml	2/3 cup
Ground hazelnuts	325 ml	1 1/3 cups
2 egg yolks		

DECORATION
Icing sugar for dusting
Jam or preserve
Piping jelly

CAKE PAN/COOKIE SHEET
Cookie sheets, well greased

BAKING
Preheated oven,
  180° C or 360° F
Middle shelf
Approximately 15 minutes, or until
  golden brown

MARY'S TIPS
Piping jelly is available from most supermarkets.
Ensure ingredients are at room temperature before mixing.

NUT MERINGUE SLICES

INGREDIENTS
Makes 16

Light brown soft sugar	60 ml	4 tbsp
Margarine	75 ml	1/3 cup
2 egg yolks		
Self-raising flour		
(see page 5)	325 ml	1 1/3 cups
Vanilla extract	5 ml	1 tsp

TOPPING
2 egg whites		
Sugar	75 ml	1/3 cup
Walnuts, chopped	30 ml	2 tbsp
Crystallized cherries, chopped	30 ml	2 tbsp

CAKE PAN/COOKIE SHEET
Shallow cake pan, 18 x 28 cm (7 x 11 ins), well greased

BAKING
Preheated oven,
180° C or 360° F
Middle shelf
20–25 minutes

MARY'S TIPS
For a good meringue, always whisk the egg whites until very stiff before adding the sugar.
Use a sterilised, grease free bowl and whisk.
Never use a wooden spoon for meringue.
Separating the eggs overnight helps the meringue to whisk stiffly.

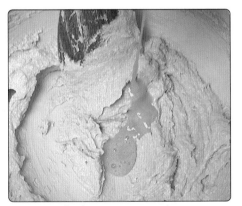

1. Cream the brown sugar and margarine together. Gradually beat in the egg yolks.

2. Sift the flour and stir into the creamed mixture together with the vanilla extract to form pastry.

3. Roll the pastry on a lightly floured surface and gently press into the base of the pan.

4. For the topping: whisk the egg whites until stiff, then add half the sugar. Whisk until very stiff.

5. Fold in the remaining sugar, chopped walnuts and crystallized cherries until evenly blended.

6. Spread the mixture over the pastry base to within 1 cm (1/2 ins) of the edges and then bake. Cut into bars while still warm, then leave in the pan until cold.

NO COOK TREATS

INGREDIENTS
Makes 28

Corn syrup	220 ml	$^7/_8$ cup
Peanut butter	250 ml	1 cup
Vanilla extract	5 ml	1 tsp
Flaked bran cereal	560 ml	2$^1/_4$ cups
Chopped peanuts	60 ml	4 tbsp

TOPPING

Dark or milk cooking chocolate	4 squares	4 squares

CAKE PAN/ COOKIE SHEET
Shallow cake pan, 18 x 28 cm (7 x 11 ins), well greased

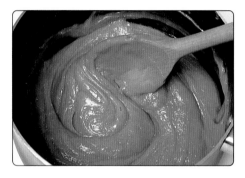

1. Mix the corn syrup and peanut butter together in a large saucepan. Cook over a medium heat stirring until mixture begins to boil.

2. Remove from the heat. Add the vanilla extract, cereal bran and chopped peanuts. Stir until well blended.

3. Spread the mixture into the prepared pan and lightly press out evenly. Chill for 1 hour.

4. Turn out on to waxed paper. Melt the chocolate (see page 15) and spread over the top using a palette knife or serrated scraper. Cut into squares when set.

ALMOND SHORTBREAD

1. Beat the butter until light and fluffy, then thoroughly beat in the sugar.

2. Lightly fold in the flour and ground rice together with the chopped almonds. Gently roll out the mixture on a lightly floured surface.

INGREDIENTS
Makes 24

Butter	125 ml	¹/₂ cup
Sugar	60 ml	4 tbsp
All-purpose flour, sifted	250 ml	1 cup
Ground rice	60 ml	4 tbsp
Chopped almonds	30 ml	2 tbsp

DECORATION
Sugar
Flaked almonds

CAKE PAN/ COOKIE SHEET
Cookie sheets, lightly greased

BAKING
Preheated oven,
   190° C or 375° F
Middle shelf
10–15 minutes, or until light brown

3. Cut out circles, then place on sheets. Press a flaked almond on top and bake. After baking, sprinkle with sugar, then leave to cool.

AUSTRIAN STREUSELS

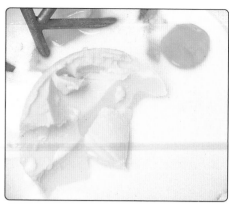

1. For the sponge cake: combine the margarine, sugar, egg, milk and flour using a beater on slow speed.

2. For the filling: mix the ingredients in a bowl to form a crumbly texture. Spread half the cake mixture into the pan, then sprinkle half the filling on top.

3. Spread remaining cake mixture on top, then cover with the remaining filling and bake. Cut into squares when cold.

INGREDIENTS
Makes 16

Soft tub margarine	75 ml	1/3 cup
Sugar	175 ml	3/4 cup
1 egg, small		
Milk	125 ml	1/2 cup
Self-raising flour, sifted (see page 5)	325 ml	1 1/3 cups

FILLING

Light brown soft sugar	75 ml	1/3 cup
Self-raising flour, sifted (see page 5)	30 ml	2 tbsp
Cinnamon	5 ml	1 tsp
Soft margarine, melted	30 ml	2 tbsp
Walnuts, chopped	60 ml	4 tbsp

CAKE PAN/ COOKIE SHEET
Square cake pan, 20.5 cm (8 ins), well greased

BAKING
Preheated oven,
170° C or 340° F
Middle shelf
35–40 minutes

MARY'S TIPS
Cinnamon is a warm, sweet, pungent spice that comes from a tree bark. It is sold as rolled dried sticks or ground.

CARAWAY COOKIES

MARY'S TIPS
Place the sifted flour lightly into your cup with a tablespoon until heaping full. Remove the excess by sliding a knife across the top.

INGREDIENTS
Makes 25–30

Margarine	75 ml	$^{1}/_{3}$ cup
Light brown soft sugar	30 ml	1 tbsp
Corn syrup	75 ml	$^{1}/_{3}$ cup
Self-raising flour		
(see page 5)	50 ml	3 tbsp
Ground ginger	2 ml	$^{1}/_{2}$ tsp
Chopped peel	50 ml	3 tbsp
Caraway seeds	15 ml	1 tbsp
Rolled oats	625 ml	$2^{1}/_{2}$ cups

CAKE PAN/COOKIE SHEET
Cookie sheets, well greased

BAKING
Preheated oven,
   180° C or 360° F
Middle shelf
Approximately 20 minutes, or until
   golden in colour

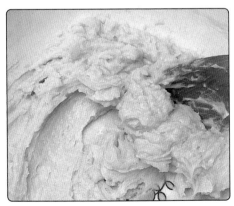

1. Cream the margarine, sugar and corn syrup together.

2. Sift the flour and ground ginger together, then place into the creamed mixture. Add the remaining ingredients and mix to a soft dough.

3. Roll out on a lightly floured surface to 6 mm ($^{1}/_{2}$ ins) thick, cut into 45 mm ($1^{1}/_{2}$ ins) diameter circles and bake. Leave to cool on wire racks.

ANISE COOKIES

INGREDIENTS
Makes 50

All-purpose flour	500 ml	2 cups
4 egg whites, small		
Sugar	250 ml	1 cup
Star anise	7 ml	1½ tsp
Pinch of baking soda		

CAKE PAN/COOKIE SHEET
Cookie sheets, well greased

BAKING
Preheated oven,
  150° C or 300° F

Middle shelf
Approximately 15–20 minutes

MARY'S TIPS
Star anise is the star-shaped fruit of a tree native to China. It has a strong liquorice-like flavour. Ground star anise is available from most large supermarkets.
This is traditionally a hard cookie.

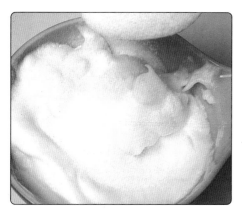

1. Sift the flour into a bowl and leave in a warm place for 10 minutes. Whisk the egg whites until thick and then fold in the sugar.

2. Mix the anise and baking soda into the flour. Fold gently into the whisked egg whites.

3. Fill a savoy bag and star tube with the mixture and pipe on to the cookie sheets. Leave to dry overnight in a warm kitchen, and then bake.

EASTER COOKIES

INGREDIENTS

Butter or margarine	125 ml	1/2 cup
Sugar	125 ml	1/2 cup
1 egg, small		
All-purpose flour	500 ml	2 cups
Mixed spice	5 ml	1 tsp
Currants	60 ml	4 tbsp
Mixed peel	30 ml	2 tbsp

DECORATION
Milk or dark cooking chocolate
Sugar
Royal icing (see page 27)

CAKE PAN/COOKIE SHEET
Cookie sheets, well greased

BAKING
Preheated oven,
    180° C or 360° F
Middle shelf
15–20 minutes,
    or until golden brown

MARY'S TIPS
Do not roll the mixture too thinly as the ears and beaks will brown quickly during baking.
Sprinkle with sugar directly after baking if cookies are not to be decorated.

1. Cream the butter or margarine and sugar until light, all-purpose and fluffy. Lightly beat the egg, then beat into the mixture a little at a time. Sift the flour and mixed spice together.

2. Fold into the mixture. Stir in the dried fruits, then knead until smooth. Place on a lightly floured surface. Roll out to 6 mm (1/4 ins) thick and cut shapes required.

3. Place even-sized shapes on the sheets, prick with a fork and bake. When cold, dip the bases into melted chocolate (see page 15) and decorate as required.

BRAN SHORTIES

INGREDIENTS
Makes 32–40

Butter or margarine	160 ml	2/3 cup
Light brown soft sugar	250 ml	1 cup
1 egg, small		
Self-raising flour, sifted		
(see page 5)	500 ml	2 cups
Natural bran	60 ml	4 tbsp

DECORATION
Icing sugar for dusting

CAKE PAN/COOKIE SHEET
Cookie sheets, do not grease

BAKING
Preheated oven,
    220° C or 425° F

Middle shelf
7–10 minutes, or until golden brown

1. Cream the butter or margarine and sugar together until soft and creamy. Then thoroughly beat in the egg.

2. Lightly fold in the flour and bran until well mixed. Place on a floured board and knead the mixture until smooth.

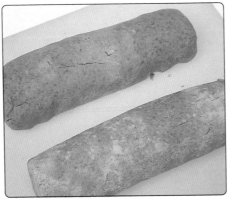

3. Divide in half and mould each into a roll 20.5 cm (8 ins) long. Wrap in waxed paper or foil and chill until firm.

4. When chilled, cut each roll into 16 or 20 slices and bake. After baking, place on wire racks to cool and dust with icing sugar.

CHOCOLATE CRACKLES

INGREDIENTS
Makes 20

Dark or milk cooking chocolate	2 squares	2 squares
Butter	60 ml	4 tbsp
Corn syrup	60 ml	4 tbsp
Sugar	60 ml	4 tbsp
Crisped rice cereal	60 ml	4 tbsp

1. Break the chocolate into small pieces. Melt the butter, corn syrup and sugar together over a low heat , then add the chocolate. Stir until melted, but do not overheat.

2. Remove from heat, then gently stir in the crisped rice cereal until well blended. Place spoonfuls into paper baking cups and leave until set.

REDBERRY FRANGIPANE

INGREDIENTS
Makes 12

All-purpose flour	310 ml	1 1/4 cups
Self-raising flour		
(see page 5)	310 ml	1 1/4 cups
Sugar	75 ml	1/3 cup
Butter, cubed	150 ml	3/5 cup
1 egg, small		
Milk	15 ml	1 tbsp

FILLING

Sugar	75 ml	1/3 cup
Butter	125 ml	1/2 cup
2 eggs, small		
Ground almonds	250 ml	1 cup
Seedless raspberry jam	60 ml	4 tbsp
Frozen cranberries	60 ml	4 tbsp
Frozen raspberries	60 ml	4 tbsp
Milk for glazing		

DECORATION
A little sugar

CAKE PAN/COOKIE SHEET
Fluted rectangular flan pan, 30.5 x 10 cm
(12 x 4 ins)

BAKING
Preheated oven,
190° C or 375° F
Middle shelf
20 minutes, then reduce heat to
180° C or 360° F
for a further 25–30 minutes

1. Sift flours together into a large bowl. Stir in the sugar, then rub in the butter until the mixture resembles fine breadcrumbs. Make a well in the centre and add the egg and milk.

2. Knead until a soft smooth dough is made. Chill for 30 minutes, then line the pan with the dough and prick with a fork. Reserve some dough for the trellis on top.

3. For the filling: cream the sugar and butter until light and fluffy. Gradually beat in the eggs and ground almonds.

4. Spread the raspberry jam over the base, using a palette knife.

5. Spread the filling over the jam. Sprinkle the frozen cranberries and raspberries on top of the filling.

6. Roll out the remaining dough and cut into narrow strips. Fix into a trellis pattern, glaze with milk and bake. Sprinkle with sugar and leave to cool in pan. Cut when cold.

CORNISH FAIRINGS

1. Sift together the flour, salt, baking powder, baking soda, mixed spice, ginger and cinnamon into a bowl. Rub in the margarine until mixture resembles breadcrumbs, then stir in the sugar.

2. Pour in the corn syrup and blend together to form a soft, smooth dough.

3. Roll the dough into walnut-sized pieces, place on sheets and bake. Do not move the sheets during baking as they may collapse if moved too early. Keep an eye on them to avoid over-colouring.

INGREDIENTS
Makes 24

Ingredient	Metric	Imperial
All-purpose flour	500 ml	2 cups
Salt	1 ml	1/4 tsp
Baking powder	10 ml	2 tsp
Baking soda	10 ml	2 tsp
Ground mixed spice	10 ml	2 tsp
Ground ginger	15 ml	1 tbsp
Ground cinnamon	5 ml	1 tsp
Margarine	125 ml	1/2 cup
Sugar	125 ml	1/2 cup
Corn syrup	125 ml	1/2 cup

CAKE PAN/COOKIE SHEET
Cookie sheets, well greased

BAKING
Preheated oven,
   180° C or 360° F
Middle shelf
7 minutes, or until golden brown

MARY'S TIPS
Don't grease a pan or sheet with margarine or butter. They contain salt that generally causes hot foods to stick.

PEANUT TRIANGLES

INGREDIENTS
Makes 20

Butter	125 ml	$^1/_2$ cup
All-purpose flour, sifted	325 ml	1$^1/_3$ cups
Light brown soft sugar	60 ml	4 tbsp
Peanuts, finely chopped	50 ml	3 tbsp

TOPPING

Peanuts, roughly chopped	60 ml	4 tbsp
Demerara sugar	50 ml	3 tbsp

CAKE PAN/COOKIE SHEET
Shallow cake pan, 20.5 cm (8 ins) square, lightly greased

BAKING
Preheated oven,
180° C or 360° F
Middle shelf
30–35 minutes, or until golden brown

MARY'S TIPS
For variation, use chopped almonds instead of peanuts. Optional topping: omit the peanuts and sugar. When cold, drizzle the tops with water icing (see page 27), or melted cooking chocolate (see page 15).

1. Rub the butter into the sifted flour until it resembles fine breadcrumbs. Stir in the sugar and finely chopped peanuts.

2. Knead the mixture well until it binds together. Press evenly into the pan, then prick with a fork.

3. Mix the peanuts and sugar together, then sprinkle on top and bake. Leave to cool for 10 minutes afterwards, then cut into triangles and leave on a wire rack until cold.

CHOCOLATE CRUNCHIES

1. Sift the flour and salt together twice. Cream the butter or margarine and sugar in a separate mixing bowl. Beat in the egg.

2. Fold in the sifted flour and salt, then fold in the chocolate pieces.

3. Mould the mixture into a long roll, and divide into 24 pieces. Place on the cookie sheets and press with a fork, then bake. Leave on sheets to cool.

INGREDIENTS
Makes 24

All-purpose flour	325 ml	1 $^1/_3$ cups
Pinch of salt		
Butter or margarine	75 ml	$^1/_3$ cup
Demerara sugar	125 ml	$^1/_2$ cup
1 egg, small		
Dark cooking chocolate cut into tiny pieces	3 squares	3 squares

CAKE PAN/COOKIE SHEET
Cookie sheets, well greased

BAKING
Preheated oven,
   180° C or 360° F
Middle shelf
10–15 minutes, or until firm

MARY'S TIPS
This is a really hard crunchy cookie. Store in an airtight container to keep crisp.

LEMON COOKIES

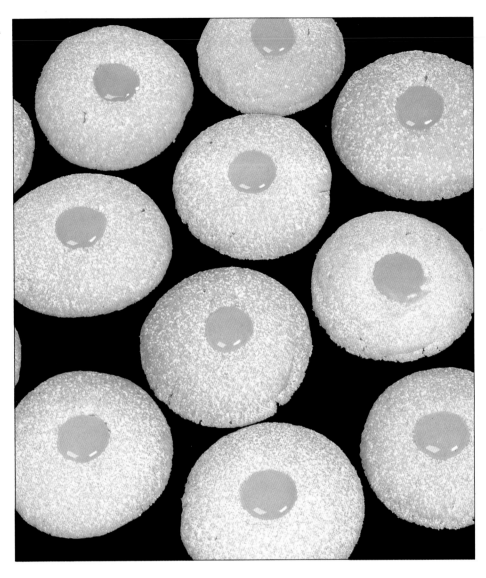

INGREDIENTS
Makes 24

Butter	75 ml	1/3 cup
Sugar	60 ml	4 tbsp
Corn syrup	15 ml	1 tbsp
Grated rind of 1 lemon		
1 egg yolk		
All-purpose flour	250 ml	1 cup
Corn starch	30 ml	2 tbsp

DECORATION
Icing sugar for dusting
Lemon curd

CAKE PAN/COOKIE SHEET
Cookie sheets, well greased

BAKING
Preheated oven,
    170° C or 340° F
Middle shelf
After 15 minutes of baking, press each top
    with the handle-end of a wooden spoon
    to form a well.
Continue baking for another 5 minutes,
    or until golden brown.

1. Cream the butter, sugar, corn syrup and lemon rind together well with a wooden spoon. Thoroughly beat in the egg yolk. Sift the flour and corn starch together.

2. Using a spatula, gradually fold in the sifted flours to form a well blended dough. Mould the dough into a roll and cut into 24 pieces.

3. Roll each piece into a ball, place on sheets and bake (see instructions above). When cold, dust with icing sugar, then fill the tops with lemon curd.

SPICED RUM COOKIES

INGREDIENTS
Makes 30

Light brown soft sugar	125 ml	1/2 cup
2 eggs, small, separated		
All-purpose flour	500 ml	2 cups
Ground cinnamon	5 ml	1 tsp
Pinch of ground ginger		
Pinch of allspice		
Pinch of ground cloves		
Sugar	75 ml	1/3 cup
Mixed peel	30 ml	2 tbsp
Grated rind of 1 lemon		
Ground almonds	60 ml	4 tbsp

DECORATION
Rum
Icing sugar for dusting

CAKE PAN/COOKIE SHEET
Cookie sheets, well greased

BAKING
Preheated oven,
   190° C or 375° F
Middle shelf
10–15 minutes, or until light brown

MARY'S TIPS
Brush the rum on while the cookies are still hot. These cookies improve with keeping. Store in an airtight container.

1. Beat the sugar and the egg yolks until light and fluffy. Sift the flour and spices together, then stir into the mixture until it resembles breadcrumbs.

2. Whisk the egg whites until they form stiff peaks, then beat in the sugar until it turns glossy. Fold into the mixture with the mixed peel and ground almonds.

3. Leave covered overnight. Roll the mixture into walnut-size pieces, place on the sheets and bake. Brush with rum and sprinkle with icing sugar while still warm.

COCONUT MUNCHIES

1. Cream the vegetable **shortening**, margarine and sugar until light and fluffy. Gradually beat in the egg a little at a time.

2. Fold in the flour and half the dessicated coconut. Add the lemon juice and mix until well blended.

INGREDIENTS
Makes 24

Vegetable shortening	75 ml	1/3 cup
Margarine	30 ml	2 tbsp
Sugar	75 ml	1/3 cup
1 egg, small, beaten		
Self-raising flour		
(see page 5)	310 ml	1 1/4 cups
Desiccated coconut	60 ml	4 tbsp
Lemon juice	10 ml	2 tsp

DECORATION
Crystallized cherries, halved

CAKE PAN/COOKIE SHEET
Cookie sheets, well greased

BAKING
Preheated oven,
   190° C or 375° F
Middle shelf
10–12 minutes, or until golden brown

MARY'S TIPS
Because vegetable shortening and lard hold less liquid, they contain the most shortening power.

3. Mould the mixture into walnut-sized pieces, then roll in the remaining coconut, place on the sheets well apart. Top each with half a crystallized cherry and bake.

MARBLED BARS

1. Blend the cocoa and hot water together and leave to cool. Place the remaining ingredients into a mixing bowl. Beat for 2–3 minutes on medium speed.

2. Divide the mixture into two equal portions. Stir the cocoa mixture into one portion until well blended.

INGREDIENTS
Makes 16

Cocoa powder	15 ml	1 tbsp
Boiling water	15 ml	1 tbsp
Soft tub margarine	160 ml	2/3 cup
Sugar	175 ml	3/4 cup
Self-raising flour		
(see page 5)	325 ml	1 1/3 cup
Baking powder	7 ml	1 1/2 tsp
3 eggs, small		

CAKE PAN/COOKIE SHEET
Shallow cake pan, 18 x 28 cm (7 x 11 ins), greased and fully lined with waxed paper

BAKING
Preheated oven,
   170° C or 340° F
Middle shelf
Approximately 25 minutes, or when firm
   to the touch

MARY'S TIPS
When cooked, this bar should spring back when lightly pressed on the top. It should also have slightly shrunk from the sides of the pan.

3. Using a dessert spoon, place alternate spoonfuls of mixture into the pan and then bake. Leave to cool in the pan for 10 minutes, then turn out on to a wire rack.

EMPIRE COOKIES

INGREDIENTS
Makes 24

Margarine	75 ml	1/3 cup
Corn syrup	60 ml	4 tbsp
1 egg yolk		
All-purpose flour	310 ml	1 1/4 cup
Corn starch	30 ml	2 tbsp
Ground cinnamon	10 ml	2 tsp

FILLING
Jam or preserve of choice

TOPPING
Water icing (see page 27)

CAKE PAN/COOKIE SHEET
Cookie sheets, well greased

BAKING
Preheated oven,
   180° C or 360° F
Middle shelf
Approximately 10 minutes, or when just
   brown around the edges

1. Thoroughly cream the margarine, corn syrup and egg yolk together.

2. Sift together the flour, corn starch and ground cinnamon, then blend into the creamed mixture to form a smooth dough.

3. Roll out thinly on a lightly floured surface, cut out with a fluted cutter and bake. When cold, sandwich together with jam. Coat the tops with feathered water icing.

CHEESE BARS

GINGER TOPPED SHORTCAKE

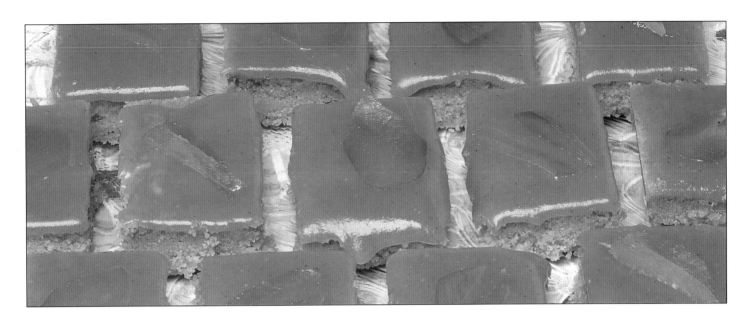

INGREDIENTS
Makes 16

Margarine	125 ml	1/2 cup
Sugar	60 ml	4 tbsp
All-purpose flour	310 ml	1 1/4 cups
Ground ginger	10 ml	2 tsp

TOPPING

Icing sugar, sifted	60 ml	4 tbsp
Ground ginger	10 ml	2 tsp
Corn syrup	30 ml	2 tbsp
Margarine	60 ml	4 tbsp
Crystallized ginger (optional)		

CAKE PAN/COOKIE SHEET
Shallow cake pan, 20.5 cm (8 ins) square, well greased

BAKING
Preheated oven,
 170° C or 340° F
Middle shelf
25–30 minutes, or until golden brown

MARY'S TIPS
Do not boil the topping too much.
Pour the topping on quickly.
Decorate with pieces of crystallized ginger for extra bite.

1. Cream the margarine and sugar together until light and fluffy. Sift the flour and ginger together, then stir into the mixture. Knead to form a smooth, firm dough.

2. Roll out and fit evenly into base of the pan, and bake. Leave to cool afterwards. For the topping: place all the ingredients into a saucepan and bring to the boil.

3. Leave to cool slightly, then spread evenly over the shortcake. Leave to set in a cold place before removing from the pan and cutting.

CINNAMON BISCUITS

INGREDIENTS
Makes 20

All-purpose flour, sifted	310 ml	1 1/3 cups
Ground cinnamon	2 ml	1/2 tsp
Unsalted butter	125 ml	1/2 cup
Sugar	60 ml	4 tbsp
1 egg, small, beaten		

TOPPING

Granulated sugar	15 ml	1 tbsp
Ground cinnamon	2 ml	1/2 tsp
Flaked almonds	30 ml	2 tbsp

CAKE PAN/COOKIE SHEET
Shallow cake pan, 18 x 28 cm (7 x 11 ins), well greased

BAKING
Preheated oven,
   170° C or 340° F
Middle shelf
Approximately 15 minutes, or until golden brown

1. Sift the flour and cinnamon together and put in a large bowl. Rub in the butter until the mixture resembles fine breadcrumbs, stir in the sugar.

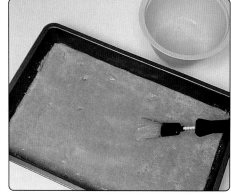

2. Place the mixture in the pan and press down to form an even base. Brush with the beaten egg.

3. For the topping: mix all the ingredients together, then sprinkle on to the base and bake. Cut into shapes while still warm.

ICED & SPICED TREATS

1. Cut the butter into pieces and place in a large bowl. Place the sugar, black molasses and spices into a saucepan and bring to boil. Add the baking soda and pour into the bowl.

2. Stir until the butter has melted, then beat in the egg. Stir in the flour. Knead the mixture to form a smooth manageable dough.

3. Roll out on a lightly floured surface to 6 mm (1/4 ins) thickness. Cut into heart shapes, place on sheets and bake. Decorate with water icing as required when cold.

INGREDIENTS
Makes 50

Butter	125 ml	1/2 cup
Demerara sugar	100 ml	2/5 cup
Black molasses	160 ml	2/3 cup
Ground ginger	5 ml	1 tsp
Ground cinnamon	5 ml	1 tsp
Ground cloves	2 ml	1/2 tsp
Baking soda	5 ml	1 tsp
1 egg, small		
All-purpose flour, sifted	500 ml	4 cups

DECORATION
1 egg white
Icing sugar (see page 27)
Various food colours
Nuts, finely chopped

CAKE PAN/COOKIE SHEET
Cookie sheets, well greased

BAKING
Preheated oven,
   170° C or 340° F
Middle shelf
Approximately 10–15 minutes, or until
   golden brown

MARY'S TIPS
Any shaped cutter can be used.
Use royal icing to add names
for a party.

APPLE SULTANA BARS

INGREDIENTS
Makes 12

Grated lemon rind	5 ml	1 tsp
Self-raising flour		
(see page 5)	500 ml	2 cups
Pinch of salt		
Corn starch	30 ml	2 tbsp
Ground cloves	2 ml	$1/2$ tsp
Margarine	75 ml	$1/3$ cup
Light brown soft sugar	75 ml	$1/3$ cup
1 egg yolk		
Milk	30 ml	2 tbsp

FILLING

Cooking apples, peeled,		
cored and sliced	1,125 ml	$4^1/2$ cups
Lemon juice	15 ml	1 tbsp
Water	30 ml	2 tbsp
Grated lemon rind	5 ml	1 tsp
Sultanas	6 ml	4 tbsp
Corn syrup	30 ml	2 tbsp

DECORATION
Icing sugar for dusting

CAKE PAN/COOKIE SHEET
Shallow cake pan, 18 x 28 cm (7 x 11 ins),
lightly greased

BAKING
Preheated oven,
220° C or 425° F
Middle shelf
Bake for 10 minutes,
then reduce heat to 190° C or 375° F,
and bake for a further 20 minutes, or
until golden brown and the pastry is
cooked through

1. For the base: sift the flour, salt, corn starch and ground cloves into a bowl. Rub in the margarine until the mixture resembles fine breadcrumbs.

2. Stir in the lemon rind and sugar, then bind to a pliable dough with the egg yolk and milk.

3. Knead on a lightly floured surface until smooth, then wrap in clingfilm and chill while making the filling.

4. For the filling: place the apples, lemon juice and water in a pan and cook gently until just tender. Remove from the heat, stir in the lemon rind, sultanas and corn syrup, then leave until cold.

5. Roll out two thirds of the dough and line the pan. Spread the filling evenly over the pastry. Roll out the remaining dough and cut into narrow strips.

6. Twist the strips as shown, using a little dab of water to fix, and then bake. After baking, dust with icing sugar. Leave to cool in the pan before cutting into slices.

CHEESEY BISCUITS

INGREDIENTS
Makes 14

Matured cheddar cheese	220 ml	7/8 cup
Salted potato chips, crushed	60 ml	4 tbsp
All-purpose flour	70 ml	5 tbsp
Icing sugar	5 ml	1 tsp
Mustard powder	5 ml	1 tsp
Pinch of cayenne pepper		
Butter	70 ml	5 tbsp

CAKE PAN/COOKIE SHEET
Cookie sheets, well greased

BAKING
Preheated oven,
190° C or 375° F
Middle shelf
Approximately 15 minutes, or until
golden brown

MARY'S TIPS
Use a strong flavoured cheese
for maximum flavour.

1. Grate the cheese into a bowl. Crush the chips lightly and mix in. Sift together the flour, icing sugar, mustard powder and cayenne pepper, and stir into the mixture.

2. Melt the butter and stir into the mixture until well blended.

3. Divide the mixture into 14 pieces, place on the sheets in small heaps and bake. Leave to cool on the sheets for 3–4 minutes, then cool on a wire rack.

APRICOT FRUIT FINGERS

INGREDIENTS
Makes 24

Whole wheat flour	175 ml	3/4 cup
All-purpose flour, sifted	250 ml	1 cup
Ground cinnamon	5 ml	1 tsp
Soft tub margarine	160 ml	2/3 cup
Corn syrup	30 ml	2 tbsp

TOPPING

Whole wheat flour	60 ml	4 tbsp
Dried apricots, chopped	310 ml	1 1/4 cups
Mixed nuts, chopped	160 ml	2/3 cup
Crystallized cherries, chopped	60 ml	4 tbsp
1 egg, large, beaten		
Orange juice, natural	125 ml	1/2 cup

CAKE PAN/COOKIE SHEET
Shallow cake pan, 18 x 28 cm (7 x 11 ins), well greased

BAKING
Preheated oven,
  190° C or 375° F
Middle shelf
Bake the base for 20 minutes,
  add the topping,
  then bake for a further 15 minutes,
  or until topping is set, but still soft.

1. Place both flours and the ground cinnamon in a bowl. Add the margarine and corn syrup.

2. Mix well to form a soft dough, then roll out and fit evenly into the pan and bake for 20 minutes.

3. For the topping: mix together the whole wheat flour, chopped fruits and nuts until well blended. Then stir in the egg and orange juice.

4. Remove the cookie base from the oven after 20 minutes. Spread on the topping evenly and bake for another 15 minutes. Leave to cool in the pan, then cut into bars.

MELTING MOMENTS

1. Cream the butter and sugar until light and fluffy. Then gradually beat in the egg.

2. Gently fold in the sifted flour. Roll the mixture on floured surface and divide into 16 pieces. Mould each piece into a ball.

3. Roll the balls in the oats to cover. Place on the sheets, flatten slightly, then bake. After baking, place half a crystallized cherry on each cookie. Leave until cold.

INGREDIENTS
Makes 16

Butter	60 ml	4 tbsp
Sugar	60 ml	4 tbsp
1 egg, small		
Self-raising flour, sifted		
(see page 5)	250 ml	1 cup

DECORATION
Rolled oats
Coloured crystallized cherries

CAKE PAN/COOKIE SHEET
Cookie sheets, well greased

BAKING
Preheated oven,
   180° C or 360° F
Middle shelf
15–20 minutes, or until golden brown

MARY'S TIPS
Take the eggs out of the refrigerator the night before so they can reach room temperature before using them. Place the balls well apart on the cookie sheets.

KATIE'S KRUNCH

1. Crush the cookies into a bowl. Sift in the icing sugar and coconut. Mix well. Melt the chocolate (see page 15). Stir the butter into the chocolate.

2. Add chocolate to the crumble mixture. Spread the mixture into the pan and chill for a few minutes. Melt white chocolate, then spread it evenly over the top.

3. Immediately sprinkle with toasted coconut. Leave in the refrigerator for 1 hour. Turn out and cut into fingers.

INGREDIENTS
Makes 28

Whole wheat cookies	250 ml	1 cup
Icing sugar	60 ml	4 tbsp
Desiccated coconut	30 ml	2 tbsp
Dark cooking chocolate	5 squares	5 squares
Butter	125 ml	1/2 cup

TOPPING
White chocolate	4 squares	4 squares

DECORATION
A little toasted desiccated coconut

CAKE PAN/COOKIE SHEET
Shallow cake pan, 20.5 cm (8 ins) square, lightly greased

MARY'S TIPS
Remember to chill the mixture for a few moments before adding the topping, otherwise the chocolate may separate when cut.

GOLDEN EYES

GOLDEN OATIES

1. Gently melt the butter with the corn syrup in a saucepan. Mix the flour, sugar, oats and ground ginger in a large bowl.

2. Stir the melted butter and the water into the dry ingredients until they are well blended.

3. Leave to cool for 5 minutes. Mould into balls, place well apart on the sheets and bake. After a few minutes, transfer the cookies on to a wire rack to cool.

INGREDIENTS
Makes 30

Butter	125 ml	1/2 cup
Corn syrup	30 ml	2 tbsp
Self raising flour	250 ml	1 cup
Light brown soft sugar	125 ml	1/2 cup
Rolled oats	310 ml	1 1/4 cups
Ground ginger	5 ml	1 tsp
Water	10 ml	2 tsp

CAKE PAN/COOKIE SHEET
Cookie sheets, well greased

BAKING
Preheated oven,
 150° C or 300° F
Middle shelf
Approximately 25 minutes

MARY'S TIPS
Measure corn syrup carefully. It will mix more readily with other ingredients if it is slightly warmed.

ORANGE BARS

INGREDIENTS
Makes 16

All-purpose flour, sifted	325 ml	1 1/3 cup
Semolina	60 ml	4 tbsp
Sugar	75 ml	1/3 cup
Butter or margarine	160 ml	2/3 cup
Finely grated rind of 1 orange		

TOPPING

Icing sugar, sifted	375 ml	1 1/2 cup
Orange juice		

CAKE PAN/COOKIE SHEET
Shallow cake pan, 18 cm (7 ins) square, well greased

BAKING
Preheated oven,
170° C or 340° F
Middle shelf
Approximately 45 minutes, or until firm to the touch.
Add the topping and bake for a further 10 minutes

MARY'S TIPS
Do not overbake the topping. Before grating, scrub the oranges to remove the wax coating. Use a coarse grater. Lemon or lime can be used instead of orange.

1. Mix the flour, semolina and sugar together in a bowl. Rub the butter or margarine into the mixture to form a breadcrumb texture. Mix in the grated orange rind.

2. Spoon the mixture into the pan. Firm down evenly with a spatula and bake. For topping: mix orange juice and icing sugar to make a thick coating consistency.

3. Spread over the cookie when baked and return to the oven for another 10 minutes. Then leave in the pan to cool before cutting.

DIGESTIVE COOKIES

INGREDIENTS
Makes 16

Whole wheat flour	170 ml	3/4 cup
Fine or medium oatmeal	50 ml	3 tbsp
Baking powder	2 ml	1/2 tsp
Pinch of salt		
Soft margarine	60 ml	4 tbsp
Dark brown soft sugar	15 ml	1 tbsp
Milk	30–50 ml	2–3 tbsp

CAKE PAN/COOKIE SHEET
Cookie sheets, well greased

BAKING
Preheated oven,
    180° C or 360° F
Middle shelf
12–15 minutes, or until just browning
    on the edges

MARY'S TIPS
For a sweet cookie, coat one
side with melted chocolate.
Comb the top as shown on
page 89.

1. Thoroughly mix the flour, oatmeal, baking powder and salt in a bowl. Rub in the margarine until the mixture resembles breadcrumbs.

2. Stir in the sugar and milk using the blade of a knife. Combine together, then knead lightly to a dough.

3. Roll out dough on a floured surface to 3 mm (1/8 ins) thick. Cut out rounds and place on the sheets. Prick with a fork and bake. Put cookies on a wire rack to cool.

INGREDIENTS
Makes 18

Margarine	30 ml	2 tbsp
Sugar	125 ml	1/2 cup
Corn syrup	75 ml	1/3 cup
Egg, beaten	15 ml	1 tbsp
All-purpose flour	60 ml	4 tbsp
Semolina	250 ml	1 cup
Cocoa powder	60 ml	4 tbsp

FILLING

Butter	125 ml	1/2 cup
Icing sugar, sifted	375 ml	1 1/2 cups
Dark or milk cooking chocolate	2 squares	2 squares

TOPPING

Sugar	30 ml	2 tbsp

CAKE PAN/COOKIE SHEET
Cookie sheets, well greased

BAKING
Preheated oven,
   180° C or 360° F
Middle shelf
15 minutes

MARY'S TIPS
To make the buttercream filling, use butter at room temperature.
Beat the butter and icing sugar together until smooth and creamy.
Flavour as required.

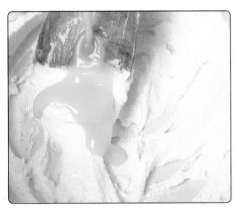

1. Cream the margarine, sugar and corn syrup together, then beat in the egg a little at a time.

2. Sift together the flour, semolina and cocoa powder, twice. Gradually fold into the creamed mixture.

3. Knead the mixture to form a smooth, well blended dough. Do not overmix.

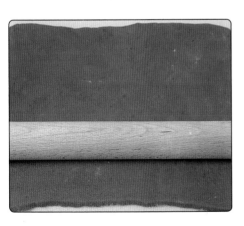

4. Gently roll out the dough into a square shape, on a lightly floured surface.

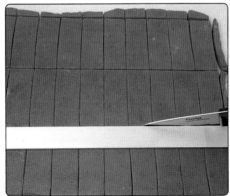

5. Using a rule, cut into even sized fingers. Prick each one with a fork, then sprinkle on the sugar. Place slightly apart on the sheets and bake. Leave until cold.

6. For the filling: beat the butter until light, then beat in the icing sugar. Quickly beat in the melted chocolate (see page 15). Sandwich the cookies together with the filling.

PARKIN

1. Sift the flour and spices together, then mix in the oatmeal. Rub in the butter or margarine until an even, crumbly mixture is achieved.

2. Stir in the sugar and corn syrup, then the baking soda dissolved in 1 tbsp of milk. Mix to a soft dough, using the remaining milk if required. Divide mixture in half and roll into a sausage shape.

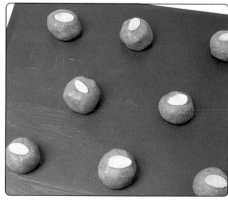

3. Cut each roll into 12 pieces. Roll into balls between floured hands and place on the sheets. Place split almonds on top, then bake. After baking, leave to cool on wire racks.

INGREDIENTS
Makes 24

All-purpose flour	325 ml	1 1/3 cups
Ground ginger	10 ml	2 tsp
Ground cinnamon	5 ml	1 tsp
Medium oatmeal	425 ml	1 3/4 cups
Butter or margarine	60 ml	4 tbsp
Light brown soft sugar	60 ml	4 tbsp
Corn syrup	160 ml	2/3 cup
Baking soda	2 ml	1/2 tsp
Milk	15–30 ml	1–2 tbsp

DECORATION
Split blanched almonds

CAKE PAN/COOKIE SHEET
Cookie sheets, well greased

BAKING
Preheated oven,
 170° C or 340° F
Middle shelf
20 minutes, or until golden brown

POLKA DOTS

1. Sift the flour into a mixing bowl, then add the butter or margarine, sugar and eggs. Beat with a wooden spoon for 4 minutes, or with an electric beater for 2 minutes.

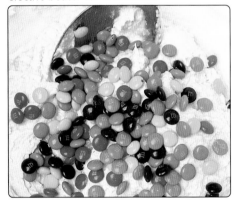

2. Fold in the coconut, vanilla extract and milk until well blended. Gently fold in the sugar-coated chocolate drops.

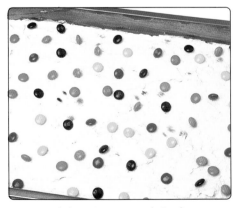

3. Spread the mixture evenly in the pan. Sprinkle chocolate drops on top and bake. After baking, leave for 2–3 minutes before turning out on a wire rack to cool. Then cut into squares.

INGREDIENTS
Makes 16

Self-raising flour (see page 5)	310 ml	1 1/4 cups
Margarine or butter, softened	125 ml	1/2 cup
Sugar	125 ml	1/2 cup
2 eggs, small		
Desiccated coconut	60 ml	4 tbsp
Vanilla extract	2 ml	1/2 tsp
Milk	30 ml	2 tbsp
Sugar-coated chocolate drops	60 ml	4 tbsp

DECORATION

Sugar-coated chocolate drops	30 ml	2 tbsp

CAKE PAN/COOKIE SHEET
Shallow cake pan, 18 x 28 cm (7 x 11 ins), greased and floured

BAKING
Preheated oven, 180° C or 360° F
Middle shelf
25–30 minutes, or until springy to the touch

MARY'S TIPS
Mix in the sugar-coated chocolate drops as quickly as possible to avoid the coloured sugar dissolving in the mixture. Chocolate chips can be used instead of sugar-coated drops.

COCONUT SQUARES

1. For the base: sift the flour into a bowl, add the margarine and rub between fingers until mixture resembles breadcrumbs. Mix in the sugar.

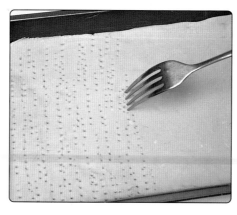

2. Add about 30 ml (2 tbsp) of water and mix with a knife. Knead to form a pastry. Roll out and fit into the pan, prick with a fork, then bake for 20 minutes.

3. For the filling: whisk the eggs, brown sugar and vanilla extract together in a bowl until light and fluffy.

4. Sift the flour, salt and baking powder together. Fold into the mixture with the coconut to form a crumbly texture.

MARY'S TIPS

Use cream cheese, icing sugar and lemon juice as an alternative topping.

When toasting coconut, watch it closely to avoid burning.

5. Spread on to the cooked base and lightly press evenly with a spatula. Bake in the oven for 10 minutes, then leave in the pan until cold.

6. For the topping: toast the coconut until golden brown. Sift the icing sugar into a large bowl, melt the margarine and stir into the icing sugar with the lemon juice.

7. Spread over the top, using a serrated scraper or fork to create a wavy pattern. Sprinkle with the toasted coconut, then cut into squares.

INGREDIENTS
Makes 24

All-purpose flour	310 ml	1 1/4 cup
Margarine	75 ml	1/3 cup
Sugar	75 ml	1/3 cup
Cold water to mix		

TOPPING

Desiccated coconut	30 ml	2 tbsp
Icing sugar	500 ml	2 cups
Margarine	30 ml	2 tbsp
Lemon juice	30 ml	2 tbsp

FILLING

2 eggs, small		
Light brown soft sugar	60 ml	4 tbsp
Vanilla extract	5 ml	1 tsp
All-purpose flour	60 ml	4 tbsp
Salt	1 ml	1/4 tsp
Baking powder	7 ml	1 1/2 tsp
Desiccated coconut	750 ml	3 cups

CAKE PAN/COOKIE SHEET
Shallow cake pan, 18 x 28 cm (7 x 11 ins),
well greased

BAKING
Preheated oven,
180° C or 360° F
Middle shelf
Bake the base for 20 minutes, or until
golden brown.
Add the filling, then bake for another
10 minutes.

COFFEE DROPS

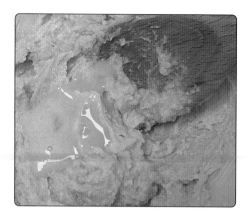

1. Cream the margarine, sugar and corn syrup together. Beat in the egg, then the coffee extract.

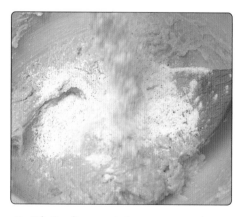

2. Sift the flour and cinnamon together, then gradually blend into the mixture to form a soft, smooth dough.

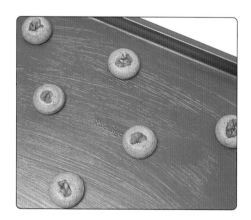

3. Fill a savoy bag and piping tube with the dough. Pipe small bulbs, placed well apart, on the sheets. Top with walnut pieces and bake.

INGREDIENTS
Makes 36

Margarine	60 ml	4 tbsp
Light brown soft sugar	60 ml	4 tbsp
Corn syrup	75 ml	1/4 cup
Egg, beaten	15 ml	1 tbsp
Coffee extract	10 ml	2 tsp
Self-raising flour		
(see page 5)	160 ml	3/4 cup
Ground cinnamon	2 ml	1/2 tsp

DECORATION
Broken walnuts (optional)

CAKE PAN/COOKIE SHEET
Cookie sheets, well greased

BAKING
Preheated oven,
    180° C or 360° F
Middle shelf
Approximately 15 minutes

MARY'S TIPS
Extra care is needed when baking these cookies as they will brown very quickly.

VIIKUNAKAKKU

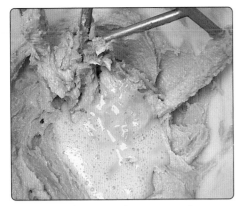

1. Beat the butter and sugar together until light and fluffy. Whisk the eggs and grated orange rind together, then gradually beat them into the mixture. Add a little flour to stop it separating.

2. Sift the flour and baking powder together twice. Mix the fruit in 30 ml (2 tbsp) of the flour and fold it into the creamed mixture. Finally, stir in the remaining flour.

3. Spread evenly in the tin and bake. After baking, leave in the tin for 10 minutes, then turn out on a wire rack to cool. When cold, dust with icing sugar and cut into bars.

INGREDIENTS
Makes 24

Butter	160 ml	2/3 cup
Light brown soft sugar	125 ml	1/2 cup
3 eggs, large		
Orange rind, grated	30 ml	2 tbsp
All-purpose flour	325 ml	1 1/3 cups
Baking powder	5 ml	1 tsp
Dried figs, chopped	70 ml	5 tbsp
Seedless raisins	70 ml	5 tbsp
Walnuts, chopped	30 ml	2 tbsp

DECORATION
Icing sugar for dusting

CAKE PAN/COOKIE SHEET
Shallow cake pan, 18 x 28 cm (7 x 11 ins), grease well, then dust with sugar

BAKING
Preheated oven,
  180° C or 360° F
Middle shelf
40–45 minutes

MARY'S TIPS
This is traditionally made in a ring mould.
Always use a very well greased pan.

GINGERBREAD SNAPS

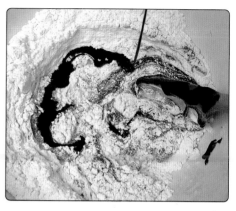

1. Put the molasses, butter and sugar into a small saucepan. Stir over a low heat until the butter has melted. Sift the remaining ingredients into a bowl.

2. When the mixture has cooled, fold into the dry ingredients to form a soft, smooth dough. Turn out and divide in half. Roll out each half to 25.5 cm (10 ins) long and cut each into 10 pieces.

INGREDIENTS
Makes 20

Black molasses	90 ml	6 tbsp
Butter	75 ml	1/3 cup
Light brown soft sugar	60 ml	4 tbsp
All-purpose flour	500 ml	2 cups
Ground ginger	2 ml	1/2 tsp
Ground coriander	2 ml	1/2 tsp
Baking soda	1 ml	1/4 tsp

TOPPINGS
Desiccated coconut
Demerara sugar
Oatmeal
Flaked almonds
Crystallized ginger pieces

CAKE PAN/COOKIE SHEET
Cookie sheets, well greased

BAKING
Preheated oven,
   180° C or 360° F
Just above middle shelf
8–10 minutes

MARY'S TIPS
When measuring the molasses, ensure it is level in the spoon with the bottom of the spoon scraped clean.
In step 1, make sure the heat is low as the mixture should melt, not cook.

3. Roll into balls and then into any of the suggested toppings. Place on the sheets and bake.

FLORENTINES

INGREDIENTS
Makes 20

All-purpose flour, sifted	175 ml	3/4 cup
Sultanas	60 ml	4 tbsp
Crystallized cherries, chopped	125 ml	1/2 cup
Flaked almonds	375 ml	1 1/2 cups
Corn syrup	125 ml	1/2 cup
Butter	70 ml	5 tbsp

DECORATION
Dark or milk cooking chocolate	8 squares	8 squares

CAKE PAN/COOKIE SHEET
Cookie sheets of appropriate sizes with paper baking cups

BAKING
Preheated oven,
190° C or 375° F
Middle shelf
10–12 minutes

MARY'S TIPS
If paper baking cups are not used, watch that the edges do not burn.

1. Mix the flour, sultanas, crystallized cherries and flaked almonds together in a bowl. Place the corn syrup and butter into a saucepan and melt.

2. As soon as the butter has melted, remove from the heat and stir in the mixed ingredients until well blended.

3. Spread small amounts into the paper baking cups or directly on the sheets and bake. Leave to cool on the sheets, then coat the undersides with melted chocolate (see page 15).

89

ALMOND & MINCEMEAT FINGERS

1. Place butter or margarine and sugar into a bowl. Separate the egg. Add the yolk to the mixture. Add almond extract, then mix to form a smooth paste. Work in all the egg white, except 5 ml (1 tsp).

2. Mix together the flour and ground almonds, then add to the mixture. Mix until a smooth pastry is formed.

3. Divide the pastry in half, roll out one half and press it into the base of the tin.

4. Spread the mincemeat on top, then the grated lemon rind.

5. Roll out the remaining pastry and lightly press over the top. Brush with the remaining egg white and sprinkle on the flaked almonds.

6. Leave in a cool place for 30 minutes. Mark into 14 fingers, then bake. After baking, gently move the fingers on to a wire rack to cool.

INGREDIENTS
Makes 14

Butter or margarine	75 ml	¹/₃ cup
Sugar	75 ml	¹/₃ cup
1 egg, small		
2 drops almond extract		
All-purpose flour	325 ml	1¹/₃ cups
Ground almonds	175 ml	³/₄ cup

FILLING
Mincemeat	325 ml	1¹/₃ cups
Grated rind of 1 small lemon		

TOPPING
Flaked almonds	30 ml	2 tbsp

CAKE PAN/COOKIE SHEET
Shallow cake tin, 18 x 28 cm (7 x 11 ins), well greased

BAKING
Preheated oven,
    180° C or 360° F
Middle shelf
Approximately 20 minutes

MARY'S TIPS
For a variation of the filling: add a little cooked apple to the mincemeat.
Or use 660 ml (2²/₃ cups) cooked apples with 60 ml (4 tbsp) of sultanas instead of the mincemeat.

MONKEY PUZZLES

1. Sift together the flour and cocoa powder twice. Cream the margarine and corn syrup until soft.

2. Stir in the flour. Coarsely crush the cornflakes and stir into the mixture until well blended.

3. Place walnut sized spoonfuls on to greased sheets and bake. When cold, dip the tops into melted chocolate (see page 15) and decorate as required.

INGREDIENTS
Makes 20

All-purpose flour	70 ml	5 tbsp
Cocoa powder	22 ml	1 1/2 tbsp
Margarine	75 ml	1/3 cup
Corn syrup	60 ml	1/4 cup
Crisp cornflakes	750 ml	3 cups

DECORATION
Dark or milk cooking chocolate, melted
White chocolate, melted

CAKE PAN/COOKIE SHEET
Cookie sheets, well greased

BAKING
Preheated oven,
180° C or 360° F
Middle shelf
Approximately 12 minutes

MARY'S TIPS
To drizzle chocolate, fill a small piping bag and cut a tiny hole at the tip. Squeeze gently and move backwards and forwards.

CRISPY OVALS

INGREDIENTS
Makes 24

2 rashers back bacon		
Whole wheat flour	220 ml	7/8 cup
Ground coriander	1 ml	1/4 tsp
Good pinch of cayenne pepper		
Butter	75 ml	1/3 cup
Matured cheddar cheese, grated	175 ml	3/4 cup
Milk	15–20 ml	3–4 tsp
Corn syrup	15 ml	1 tbsp
Milk for glazing		

TOPPINGS
Sesame seeds
Poppy seeds
Parmesan cheese, grated

CAKE PAN/COOKIE SHEET
Cookie sheets, well greased

BAKING
Preheated oven,
190° C or 375° F
Middle shelf
10 minutes, or until lightly browned

MARY'S TIPS
Other savoury toppings could be used, such as anchovies or roasted chopped peppers. For cocktail crackers, use a small cutter. These cookies make an excellent base for hors d'oeuvres.

1. Derind the bacon, cut into pieces and fry until very crisp. Drain on kitchen paper. Sift the flour, coriander and pepper together, then mix in the butter forming a crumb texture.

2. Chop the bacon finely. Add to the mixture with the cheese. Mix together to form a pliable dough, adding milk as required.

3. Roll out the dough on a surface dusted with whole wheat flour. Cut into fluted ovals and place on the sheets. Brush with milk, sprinkle on various toppings and bake.

CHRISTMAS COOKIES

1. Place the butter or margarine, sugar, sifted flour, milk and corn syrup into a bowl. Mix the ingredients together, using a wooden spoon or electric beater, until it forms a soft dough.

2. Turn out on a lightly floured surface and knead. Gently roll out the dough and cut shapes as required.

3. Place on the sheets and bake. After baking, leave for 5 minutes, then cool on wire racks. Decorate using chocolate for feet and royal icing for the snow.

INGREDIENTS

Soft tub margarine		
or butter	125 ml	1/2 cup
Sugar	160 ml	2/3 cup
All-purpose flour,		
sifted	500 ml	2 cups
Milk	50 ml	3 tbsp
Corn syrup	15 ml	1 tbsp

DECORATION
A little royal icing (see page 27)
Dark or milk cooking chocolate, melted

CAKE PAN/COOKIE SHEET
Cookie sheets, well greased

BAKING
Preheated oven,
   190° C or 375° F
Middle shelf
15 minutes, or until pale golden in colour

MARY'S TIPS
Do not overknead the dough, or the cookies will be tough. Wrap the cookies in coloured foil and hang on the Christmas tree.